T0021686

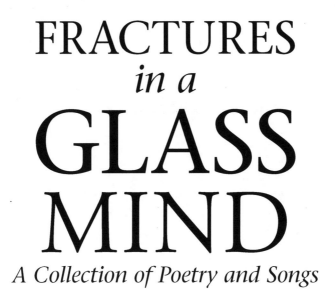

FRACTURES
in a
GLASS
MIND

A Collection of Poetry and Songs

Nicholas C. A. Sparkman

FRACTURES IN A GLASS MIND
A COLLECTION OF POETRY AND SONGS

iUniverse books may be ordered through booksellers or by contacting:

iUniverse
1663 Liberty Drive
Bloomington, IN 47403
www.iuniverse.com
1-800-Authors (1-800-288-4677)

ISBN: 978-1-5320-6516-3 (sc)
ISBN: 978-1-5320-6517-0 (e)

Library of Congress Control Number: 2019900564

Print information available on the last page.

iUniverse rev. date: 02/21/2019

To my mother, who nurtured my creativity and passion.
To my father, who structured it.
To my siblings, who support it.
To my friends, who instilled it.
For my wife, who gives me the courage to use it.

Card House

The black smoke rises.
It bellows through
This house of cards
That sways from side to side.
These faces haunt me
As memories are retold that reveal me
In a most unfamiliar light
And open me up to the ugliness of my world.
So I shut it all away.
I will not expose my heart.
I cannot free my mind,
For the world grows colder
And the wind blows bolder,
Until I see the cards fall away.

The smoke begins to thicken
So much that cards cannot be recognized
As they descend
Ever so slowly
And I am left with uncertainty.

So one by one,
By ace, by king, by queen,
Even though my body is reduced to ash,
Even though my memories remain intact,
I continue building,

To enclose the things I'd rather forget,
Until my house of cards,
Filled with black smoke,
Falls back down again.

Gaslighting

All you ever wanted
Was all I ever needed,
Just your arms around my neck,
My hands around your waist.
We've seen what the world can really do,
Breaking innocence by following through
With its cruel intentions invading your eyes.
Now all I see is blue. No, all I see is you.
All I ever wanted

Was all you ever needed,

Someone to talk to late at night,

Someone to tell me it's all right.

Now the words just end in fights.
I can't leave it at "It didn't matter."
But it really sounds so much sweeter
Than watching this love fall apart,
Because love like this is bound to.
All we ever wanted,
All we ever needed,
My hands around your neck now,
Your claws are in my waist now.
We've thrown it all away.

God's Movie Theater

The man sits in his dark room.
The projector clicks as it reels and spins.
It projects an explosion of a billion brilliant pixels
Onto the dark room's wall.
This man sees them all at once,
Smiling and crying as the scenes fade in and out.
In each pixel a picture of life:
Lives lived well,
Lives destroyed,
Lives of faith and prosperity,
And those of loss and unjustified madness.

He watches in a vicarious state
Reminiscent of a time
When he himself directed this giant multifilm
When it was a theater for his own unique amusement,
Getting involved when characters made him curious
Or, more often, when they made him furious,
Throwing tantrums onstage or adding props and plot twists
Whenever he fancied it necessary
For his own self-righteous enjoyment.

Then, finally, the characters took to themselves
In their own scenes,
In their own time.
With this insult he grew tired of direct intervention

And bestowed upon the stage

The only lead the world would ever need,

The character that would set the motion for everything after to come.

He expected change but not in the way the story evolved.

The actors continued to fight for their moment

In his big picture, in the world.

And because of this, he walked out of his dark room

And stayed away for a very, very long time,

Dissatisfied with the fact that his true vision would never be seen.

And away he went, leaving all of it behind,

Until the curiosity crept in him again and his son beckoned his eyes

Toward the light of the projector once more.

So now he sits in his dark room pondering,

Watching his billion pixels as they live and struggle and die.

All the while the bigger picture unfolds,

And it finds him confounded,

Because he, like us, has no say over the outcome.

He ponders this and smiles and pulls out a small reel he keeps on his person,

Ready to splice in at any moment

A reel labeled "Armageddon."

With his great climax already directed,

The suspense for the end begins to boil.

One day he will be ready to end his masterpiece.

And then, when the people pray to him,

He'll hear them true and mutter,

"I have already saved you."

His will is done.

Now he watches it unfold,

A spectator only.

In and out of the room he walks,
Disgusted with the things he sees,
Beckoned back to direct by the faith he requires to breathe.

There is beauty in the pictures
As the projector clicks and spins.
He is too busy watching and lazing,
Bingeing his pixelized light.
A billion pixels.
God watches them all.

Perfection

There you stand,
    Looking in my direction,
  Demanding my perfection.
        My thoughts are your collection.

        I cannot,
        I will not,
        I cannot stand
      To have you giving out an open hand
            While this heart is in such high demand
            Until my blood is made of nothing more than

sand.

                Breathing in my complications,
      Here you are in your perfection,
                Standing in the way of my

direction,

                Acting as though I am your creation, as if
        These words of mine are your collection.

Skew

A skewed perception of time,
    Of a life that feels like it's not mine.
        Circumstance held by the power of fate.
            It seems to me it all comes far too late.

Seconds, minutes, hours, days,
    All blurred together in a frenzied haze,
        Spinning, surging, and slurring together,
            A skewed perception of forever.

Chaos is a privilege
    Called upon to be a bandage
        When the mundane takes over.
            Life is nothing like a four-leaf clover.

Luck is a commodity,
    While patience is the joke,
        An illusion in the making
            When thoughts are no longer provoked.

With this much said, I wait
    For an altered point of view,
        Entertaining no longer
            A time and life askew.

Empathy

Mystery in an emotion.
To feel what another does.
So many, so reckless, so vivid,
Yet defused to control the situation.

Walk a mile in these shoes.
Feel the wear; feel the use.
It may be useless, but it's true.
I can feel just like you.

I can feel the pain.
I can feel the hurt, the bruises,
The imprints that someone else uses
To get to you and so to get to me.

If eyes are just a window,
Your face is an open door,
Opened to empty space,
Opened to a home without a place.

I can feel just like you.
I can see the things you do.
But how can I expect to heal
If you won't follow through?

You're a mystery in motion.
I wish you could explain the notion
Of why I feel like such a bore.
Because I can't bear to be you anymore.

Asleep

When I sleep,
I search my dreams
For the resemblances of you.
They crash like the water
Of a thousand seas,
Flooding every inch of me.
It fills me to the point that
I wake up afraid and screaming,
Exhausting what little I have left.
This hollow shell.
Knowing I can't be filled the same,
I drudge through the day
Awake, but not here,
Regretting the night I spent,
Dreading the visions of you,
Conflicted that I want them to
Burn every nerve within
Like the fires engulfing a forest.
I am left alone
In this pain,
Not awake,
Not asleep,
Just alive,
Dreaming   of you.

Frets

Another finger on another fret.
Some lipstick on that cigarette.
Breaking words like breaking news,
Singing flaws while shaking the blues.
Blood runs slow
Off my fingertips.
Blue moons glow
From your sun-kissed lips.
Fresh-spun webs
From a midnight kiss,
Something to scratch
As a cure for the itch.

Lungs collapse as a heart breaks.
Body falls as my bones shriek.
Swing life as if we're all on rope.
Letting go in fear, I hope.
But these stars were meant for you,
My dear.
These clouds were meant for me.
Hold me closer before you let go.
Fear is something I'll never know.

Living life in a cutthroat way,
Burning up, cutting into the fray,
You justify my mental state,

But that's not something up for debate.
Blood runs slow
From your fingertips.
Blue suns glow
Off my moon-kissed lips.
Fresh-spun webs
On this midnight trip
Stealing your scratch
As a cure for my itch.

Praying for some peace of mind.
None coming from a God so kind.
Just the devil in my head playing you.
And it's a curious bet
As another finger meets another fret.

Voices

They keep telling me it's time.
Just simply go and draw the line
Between what's here and there
Just to make it through.

These voices in my head
Tell me it's okay to live,
And if it were up to me,
I'd follow through.

But the things I do and say
Are always getting in the way,
Making me wonder if
You were ever never true.

I can't wait for this to just be through.
I remember all the lines that you drew,
And now I belong to something
So much better than you.

It's time to cross the line.
Voices tell me that it's time
To go and live my life.
Never better than I've been without you.

Intention

Doubt rains down
From the summer sky,
Things I should have said
But instead did deny
Like I didn't care,
Walking straight for winter air.
Forgive my intention.
You took my lies for truth.
I asked for this tension.
I tried to hide it too soon.
Now I'm on the cold hard ground,
And I realize I am not immune.
If the summer's this cold,
I won't survive the winter.
Even the summer's hot glow
Can't warm a heart so bitter
Now, when everyone turns away.
Why must this go on another day?
Once a friend,
Now break, now bend.
Once a sister,
Now tear, now fray.
If the summer's this cold,
I won't survive winter's first day.

Alone

Lately I've been talking to myself
Because I don't have anybody else.
In this head of mine I ponder
Why being social is so somber.
God, I wish I was at home
So I could pass the hours in my room

Alone.

I'm doing my best
To keep my wicked mind at rest,
But somehow I'm caught up in this mess
Of giving all, receiving less.
It's something I've got on my chest,
When all I want to do
Is to scream at home
In my room.

I don't want to be …
Alone.

These voices in this head of mine,
They whine and reach and claw and climb,
Because there's something in the words I say
That make them all crawl out to play.
And once they're out, they're quite the bitter friends,

But I stick with them and speak to them
In my room at home
Because I'm just so …

Alone …

Lately I've been talking to myself
Mainly because I have nobody else.
In this prison of mine I am stagnant,
Waiting for connection to be rendered.
But sure enough, no dial tone
While I'm trying to call me
In my room, so …

Alone.
I can't take it anymore.

I've got obligations,
Bills and tills I really have to pay.
They all just get up in the way
Of all the things I want to do and say.
It's like being stuck in the mud
When I'd rather be at home,
Clean, in bed, inside my room,

Alone.
I can't live like this anymore.

Looking down at all these
Memories
Like pictures in a book of
Prophecies,
I can't take another look.

Alone,
I feel like I'm drowning.
Alone.
It's time to act
Alone.
I guess I'll never know
Why I've always felt so ...

Alone.

A Good Cause

Caught in the wake of a stupefying madness in relation to a cause I no longer see as my own, I am awake enough to see the so-called glory the ones around me seek. But I find in it neither hope nor any joy.

My mind is never here. It's always away in a more suitable environment where people think differently, where the thought is not on what is at hand but on what is at the hands of those who love me. The people who are in my reality, they talk of war and destruction, a game they have made to fulfill the ideal of freedom. I hear the cry of orders to put together a machine of war, but I have also heard the cry of men's bodies at the burden.

I have been trained to follow, and yet they expect me to lead, and thereby, somehow, they also expect a slave. Even as I slumber, though, I am of more conscious mind.

This uniform bears on it a particular burden, one I have yet to feel accustomed to. The burden of a contract signed in negligent youth. The burden of useless and endless hours gone by. The burden of political deficiencies and a lack of regard for common sense. In these burdens I see my wasted youth trickling to the floor like the water from a washcloth being squeezed dry to suit someone else's purpose.

I am tired now.

I awake only out of a regard for consequences I do not want to see come upon myself. And I find it humorous because I am no longer myself. I am lost behind the daydreams of what and where I could be had I not raised my right hand that fateful, painful day. I did not know that that day would be the last day I would have a voice, the last time I had a choice.

Promises of a better day on the same agenda wrack and tatter my ears. They speak of gaining respect because of an extra piece of cloth sewn onto their collars, under the illusion that they are not in a trap, a trap that pulls you in with the promise of an extra stripe or ribbon that will make you a better man than the next. Yet under this trap there are too many who are convinced, too many for me to fight alone.

So, I must bide my time and either let the illusion sway me into its clutches or continue fighting those who'd die for nothing. This has become my cause. Unfortunately, there is no room for others.

Wings

Good faith dies.
A feeble mind weeps and cries.
I am desperate in the mornings.

                                        Will my will survive?

Into the ice-cold,
My fortune to be told.
And I could be none the wiser.

                                        Rather that than to be lonely.

Is that better?
To know that I am self-made?
And yet to still wake up feeling …

                                        Manufactured and ordained.

Resting only to accomplish
The physicality to abolish
A resolve to be submissive,

                                        Consciousness to which I am inclined.

The story is told
About the wings of the bold,
How their heaps of people will follow.

As I just wait in bed for tomorrow,

I cannot wait to think and strive
For my mind and body to feel alive
And for everyone I know looking toward me.

Admiration destroys humility.

I turn over on my side, groaning.
Lucky me,
Another morning.

Will my will survive?

Scatterbrained

Bubblegum trees

In the middle of some asphalt.

Broken hearts in the dust

from the breeze

While we live and travel.

I can't help but stutter now

As the words come up as vomit.

Going around in circles, dizzy.

Yes, I'm a little unstable

As I'm a little scatterbrained
And a little fucking rattled.
Knees freshly scabbed
Coming straight up off the gravel.
Hearts crisscrossed
In a never-ending battle.

I have no idea where to go.
I'm lost inside my mind, and so
                    I go outside to see things for myself.
And the sight is overwhelming ...

I see bubblegum trees
In the middle of some asphalt.
Knees get meek,
And they watch me unravel.
I didn't pay for the show;
I paid for Elavil!

                                                    Ha!

        Soft white coats and alibis.
                Trying to bite the ends that are tied.
I'm just going around in circles, dizzy,
                  Begging my thoughts to be more verbal

                          Because I'm a little scatterbrained.
                              I'm a little fucking rattled.
Thought my feelings were aloft.
                Turns out it was just the fucking Zoloft!

        Ha!

Cold black jackals
Pull me into my grand white casket.
The joke is on them, however.
I'll never be lonesome
In this comfy straitjacket.

Limbic

I love the fall, but it smells a lot like reminiscence,
A recollection of all things clairvoyant,
A recall of memories you take from a spot on your bedroom wall,
Looking at all the things you missed before,
Sitting there reminded that things have changed.

I'd love the winter, but the cold just feels so much like longing.
The songs that take me there are worse than the way the weather stings.
I wish I enjoyed the December air, but it reminds me of that expedition,
The one I took so long ago when things would never change.

Bring on spring. It smells of sweet nostalgia,
Before the things we did were contemplated,
A time when the sun rose in my mind and the moon with my body.
The smell, the feel, the hope, reverse, return, rewind.
It's laid out before me that change is something to be intertwined.

I love the summer because it's nothing but thoughtful memories.
The best of times and the worst of newfound emotion.
The late-night talks, the early morning walks, and the drives we always
took.
The sunrise, the sunset, the moon, the stars.
Every time I see them, they remind me
They are never going to change.

Stop

These words won't come out right.
Looking at pictures.
Not sure how I feel.

Things are changing
In drastic ways.
I feel as though I'm left behind.

I know what I'd like to say, but the words get mixed up.
I end up on a different page,
In a different mood.

The world needs the people I know.
How big is their part to play?
How big is mine?

How do I impact the world from where I stand?
Who am I to make a difference?
In the next eighty years I'll be gone anyway.

Living in memory has a ring to it,
Yet part of me finds immortality interesting,
After the first century, of course.

I'm given an opportunity to move
After seven long years of wanting to get out.
Now I find it hard to leave.

My motivation has dropped quite rapidly.
I don't know what to do with myself
It's 3:00 a.m., and I'm not even tired.

Hence, I'm writing this just to see my thought process
Stop ...
Anyway, back to the point:

I miss people,
But ... I have enough here.
I want to connect with some old friends and don't know how.

I should be asleep,
Not here on Facebook with bloodshot eyes,
Torturing myself with pictures that are painful to see.

I'd love to write a well-written poem about it, but, like I said,
The right words won't come out, so I'm typing and typing and typing and
typing.
My phone just rang.

I had hoped it was a friend wondering what I was up to.
Nope, just a Facebook update on some stupid spammer who just tried to
add me.
Goddammit.

I think I'm done ranting for now.
Time for a cigarette,
Then bed hopefully. Stop ...

No Other

Your voice is the thing that keeps me from going crazy.
Your lips keep me off the edge.
Your eyes are the sunshine when I'm feeling low,
Illuminating me with your perfect glow.
I can't explain or make it show
How amazing you are.

I can try though.

When I'm in my darkest hour,
There's just no point in prayer.
I think about your gorgeous face,
And the rest just disappears.
I'm sorry for the times I doubted,
All the bullshit I pursued.
But now I know there can't be—no,

Not—another you.

So, I'm sold.
You have my heart,
And there's nothing
You can do,

Because there is
No other me,
And there is

No other you.

Blind

I had a dream the other day,
But not one of which you may think.
It was one where sight was of no use,
Just one of instinct and feeling.
Think of going blind, or rather of saving your mind
From the pain you see every day,
Relying on your other senses only,
Creating an imagined world around you,
Blind to judgment of appearances,
Blind to a world that can see you,
No longer afraid of vision,
No longer a slave to sight.
Seeing the world has new meaning.
The world and its people,
All just voices, scents, and feelings.
"More than meets the eye" would no longer apply.

Colors

Lightning shoots the sky.
It takes my breath away.
Black goes white.
Sound bites the ground.
Shocks are left to stay.

Fill my heart with colors;
Fill my head with joy.
Watch the sunset break away my inhibitions.
Let the night shape over some new ones.

Rain hits the ground.
The world begins to overflow.
My mind begins to burn to ashes
With my body, bones, and soul.

Fill my head with colors;
Fill my heart with pain.
Watch the nightmare fade away.
The sunrise starts a brand-new day.

I stop to take the beauty in.
Before the colors bleed and fade,
Before the storm begins to swirl and spin,
I close my eyes to let the colors in.

Fill my eyes with color;
Fill my hands with bliss.
Watch the world come to life
As the storm clouds stand motionless.

I am nothing more
Than what I am today,
And all I know is that even after it all,
I will never let these colors fade to gray.

Fly

I'll fly into your room,
Watch you cry,
Watch you sleep,
Watch you heal.
But attached to the wall, I feel,
Is less than you deserve.

When will it be over?
When will you become yourself again?
Your heart's been broken.
Through it all, I've lost my friend.

You kick and scream.
You awake from dreams.
I watch it all unfold.
Get back up; you'll be okay—
As if it helps at all.

When will it be over?
Will it ever end?
Where's the friend I thought I knew?
Will I ever be myself again?

Ellipses

Dot. Dot. Dot.
I can't handle my thoughts.
Becoming distraught.
Pretending that I am well taught.
Smiling and
Talking and
Smiling,
When inside I'm screaming.

Presenting this face
I wish to erase.
Walking fast-paced.
Still losing the race.
Walking and
Running and
Sprinting,
When I can't catch up,

I refuse to lose,
But now I must choose
To pick up these clues
Or wallow in the blues.
Searching and
Finding and
Losing again,
When, I know I have failed.

Dot. Dot. Dot.
I'm cutting the knot,
The very reason for which I have fought.
They've kept my blood in a clot,
And now that it's not …
I just keep on bleeding.
Bleeding and
Bleeding and
Bleeding.
When I wish I had learned

That when something is burned,
The pain of that something is earned.
The debt of regret comes with it
When I learn how to bear it.

…

Can you hear me screaming?
Can you feel me losing?
Can you see me bleeding?
Can you smell me burning?

Dot … Dot … Dot …

Sunshine

Take a look around.
It's cloudy down here every day.
The sunshine's blocked,
And it's not okay,
Because on the other side
Is where the other angels go to play,
Blocked by a gray wall
Every day.
Simple sunshine
In a sullen place.
My Mother Nature side
Is crawling out at its own pace.
So, I ask again,
Will you fly with me?
Or end up wishing you had come
To the place we cannot see?
Jumping on the clouds
Like pillows,
No longer in the shrouds,
No longer in their shadow.

Insular

Stuck on this island,
Oh and I'm here to stay.
As the world around me turns,
Morphing like clay,
I stay the same.
And while I know I'm not perfect,
I know that I deserve it.
Please, just find another way.
Take me with the undertow.
Throw me with the waves
With those who are my family, my friends.
This world keeps moving.
I can see it as it moves.
From this island I see you.
I just wish you could see me too.
I am a menace to myself.
I am reminded every day.
So sorry to have poisoned you
In such a clever killing way.
I am here by choice,
Signed in blood, signed in vain.
This is how I hurt myself
To make up for your pain.
I hope I'm far enough away that
You can leave me behind.
Just think about your future now.

Don't let me cross your mind.
Stuck on this island,
Watching all your days go by,
I know I'll never make up for it,
So why even try?

Vigilia

I cannot sleep tonight.
Thoughts are far too loud,
Doubts and suspicions
Fogging like a cobweb.
No room left for me, for
Calm and peace of mind.
These thoughts break the silence.
I cannot sleep tonight.
Tell the world I'm sick of you.
Tell them all I never followed through.
See what lies inside this curse,
This chaotic state of mind
That keeps me longing
For a better time.
Lonely doesn't cut it.
A form of solitude I seek.
No room left for those who followed
Into the hell I have achieved.
Now is not the time for sleep.

Fear the wandering mind, for it only exists in tragedy. While the mind wanders, it looks for possibilities. The possible is only attained when there can be possibility. When there are no more possibilities, you are fully satisfied. Therefore, when you are happy, you are satisfied, and your mind no longer wanders. That is, unless you are never satisfied. If you are never satisfied, you will never know happiness. The cold fact is that sadness knows no bounds, while happiness can only last for so long. So rather than despise tragedy, welcome it. Welcome it to learn. Welcome it to strive. Welcome it, and let it consume you, but not to the point of insanity, no. Unless you are one who can control how far to go, do not let your mind wander too far, or you will undoubtedly lose your soul.

Ghosts

We can hear them singing.
We can hear them calling.
They're bottled up
And crying out,
Waiting for us to face them.
Just faces from a past
We've pushed aside.
Moved on but never gone.
Passive-aggressive in their nature.
We can see it in their pictures.
Burning holes with old eyes
We've tried so hard to forget,
And yet they still linger inside.
I saw a figure today,
And its shadow followed me
As if faded memories
Looking through the broken glass.
The floor moves.
The walls shake.
Until peace is made,
They may not fade.
They are here to haunt us.
As time goes on,
We will join them.

Tameshigiri

It's been awhile since I've cried in that way.
That helps heal the cuts from a bad yesterday.
It's been awhile since I've screamed with no one around
Just to see if I'd be heard.

Sleep never comes.
I'm still wide awake,
For dreams are unwelcome here,
As is the thought of you.

And yet the fact remains
That when the ground gives way beneath my feet,
I'd rather you fall with me
Than feel that surge of abyss alone.

You cut me to the point
That I'm on my knees.
Suffering you is something
That's always fine by me.

I'm always awake.
It's fine by me.
Keep cutting
So I know you're still there.

If it makes you feel better,
If the cuts make you feel stronger,
I'll take them as they come
Just to show I still care.

But when my body is done,
When I can bleed no more,
Look me in the eyes and lie,
Because I know you won't fall with me.

And there's nothing I can do about it.
It's just the way I am.
Just as long as you're cutting *me*,
I'll take it until you let me stand.

Just don't let me fall alone.
I'll bleed out before I do.
But if the ground gives way beneath you,
I'll let the world take me too.

Closer

I want to be closer
To you and the words you gave me,
Standing as a child in your grace,
Only to walk on my own at a faster pace.
It's amazing what a year can do.
It's unbelievable what the world can't.
No, I'm not who I used to be,
But if I could go back, I would.
Compassion is my nature.
Thrown about into a town no one knows,
No one knows what good I can do.
Everyone tends to see the bad.
It's not a plea I'm putting out,
Nor a submission.
I'm stuck in the middle here.
All I see is a petty obsession.
War isn't fair,
But neither is love.
We can try to choose,
But the choice lies somewhere else.
Writing words never seemed so difficult.
Feelings transgressed into language,
Weaving through sovereign emotions,
Never wanting to see the light again.
Change is something hard to do.
With the right motivation it's possible.

All I know is that mine lies in you.
Whether or not you choose to accept it,
I want to get lost in you.
Take me back to a simple manner.
You're better than I was years ago.
I want to feel like that again.
Maybe it's a complicated request.
What's done is done.
I cannot change that.
But for now,
All I want is to be closer to you.

Moonlight

The moon shines bright
Every night,
In every way
Full of imperfection,
But still perfect in every way.

Forgive me if I stare.
I can no longer hold it at bay.
To see the light!
Look at it shine.
It's better than the sun that lights day.

I know this won't make perfect sense,
But while I've shown enough petty ignorance,
I still keep thoughts on tomorrow,
Dreaming to keep it at bay.
I sleep throughout the day

So I can see her majesty shine.
In such contrast to the black that holds her,
Her beauty shines in every way.

As sunlight breaks,
I feel it burn with its horrible ray.
I hate that there's no mystery left in the day.

I'm sick of feeling shallow.
I'm hanging onto the moon, even if I must from the gallows.

Why grip into someone's solemn teeth in plain light?
Why feel the bite of a shadow when you can roam free at night?
Why squander every want, every need, every right?
Why use the black when the moon shines bright?

Euphoria

Hints of a child wander through the hallways,
Looking at and examining the new you,
Screaming, "Who are you?"
To which you reply, "I am you, and there's nothing you can do."

Nostalgia in the air.
This game just isn't fair.
Watching time go by; it slowly slips away.
Seeing vividly as things grow gray,
As a sense of madness creeps into your heart.
And now you wish you could still have a part

Of that child in the air.
Haunting you, now it's forever dear
As it wanders through your hallways,
On your walls, and in your heart.

You realize now that reality is real.
There's no going back
Until your body lies in the crematoria.
Your heart and mind won't get back to euphoria.

The Spider

As I stand as a playful child catching bugs in a jar, waiting for the moment to strike so that my friend in the corner can have his meal, I open the lid and watch them fly, just to be caught in the web—just so I may watch them die.

I see him come down and smile as they struggle. Oh, how they fight. No hope is there for them, and they will never fly again. He bites and lets the poison sink in, and I think, *What a courtesy for the struggling dead.* Almost like euthanasia. They finally stop squirming, and this disease begins its work.

He wraps them in what caught them until they suffocate. He then pulls them into his nest, where they wait to be devoured. Like a body to be buried. No funerals here, however. They will never see the light again. And I realize now that as a boy, I watched, amazed by their defeat.

I realize now that I, too, will never see the light again. Because you've opened the lid and you've watched me fly right into this trap, this trap you knew was ahead of me. Nature is fair after all.

Without Answer

A question.
It's in the mind.
It's in the soul.
Why do we hurt ourselves?
Of this no one will ever know.

Things said in the past tense.
Things of peace we still can't mend.
Why do we kill ourselves over what's happened?
Of this I will never know.

The screams of war in a quiet mind.
The words are thought but never said.
Why do we fail to communicate?
Of this I will never know.

Why we dream of better days,
Why we bicker in adolescence,
Why we cannot go back in time.
Of this I will never know.

It's an art
To fall apart.
Why are we not all together?
Of this I will never know.

We cannot move on.
We live in the dream.
Why can't we let go?
Of this I will never know.

Blank in emotion,
Numb to the touch.
Why do we use anger as a weapon?
Of this I will never know.

Life, it goes on,
No matter the trifle or the fight.
Why don't we see we are breathing and alive?
Of this I will never know.

I'm sick of this way,
Ignorant and unwilling to stay.
This secluded arrangement
That makes up my day.
Sleep makes sense,
But to waste the day doesn't seem right.
But here I am awake,
And it's almost daylight.

I can't help but think.
My understanding heightens at night,
For the sun blinds my thoughts,
And activities cause me to lose sight.
It's not a plea or a complaint.
It's just a note I'm willing to take.
And as sleep nears,
Dreams swallow my fears.

But take a moment to think.
It's not often we do,
Unless someone we know is hurting,
Or unless we are too.
Think of what life is to you.
Is it watching bad things happen and letting them slide?
Is it being the one people seek out in whom to confide?
Is it trying to decide what person you're willing to be?
Whatever your path, just know
Life is full of tragedy.

Protect it and endure,
For life is the only thing worth waiting for.
It may not start at the age of five,
But cherish the thought of being alive.
The thought fits like a glove.
When the dark was the only thing to be afraid of,
Think back to the days before the formidable slumber,
When eyes were open and the world was a wonder.
Think of when it was simple,
When you could always best your foes.

It's not a question but an answer
To the world that's become bland,
Colors fading.
Seek the rhythm and the band.
Seek to be a little wild.
Seek out the eyes of a child.
Back when bedtime was bedtime
And breakfast was always waiting early,
Back when the ride to school was always a journey,
When your parents were always flirty.
Dream of things that have passed.

Therefore, I sleep
To stay out of reach of the future's grasp.
Just give me one more day
In a perfect past.

Like I Do

All these people
Wallowing around me,
They didn't ever know you
Or miss you like I do.
They never felt the warmth of your breath
Or smelled the scent of your hair.
They can never lose you or love you like I do,
Never like I did.
I cannot deny it;
I feel spited,
Like a little kid on the floor
In the corner of make-believe and life.
You were the key to my strife.
And I swear they'll never love you like I did,
Like I did.
You were the beginning of my happiness.
You were the end of my sadness,
And now you're the beginning of my madness.
No, they'll never miss you
Like I do.

Let Us Pray ...

Dear Lord, thank you for this day.

Thank you for the food before us that you so graciously enabled us to provide for ourselves.

Because ultimately, you alone are the reason we can.

Tonight, we pray to you for our families and the struggles that you lay before them.

We pray for the pregnant mother of three who lies awake at night, wondering where her husband is.

We pray for the unfaithful husband who is in turmoil because his wife has been unfaithful as well.

We pray for their children as they cower in the corner and cover their ears to shield themselves from the vulgar screams.

We pray that your plan, O mighty God, will not affect them negatively.

We pray for the divorce that brings peace to the family even though you frown upon it.

We pray for the alcoholism and drug abuse that comes to follow when that mother finds herself destroyed by the path you laid before her.

We pray for the youngest who will not hear until the age of three because his parents were so busy fighting that they couldn't recognize that their child wasn't speaking.

We pray for the preacher whom you allow to play friend in your house while he molests women who are under his employment,

For allowing him to destroy their credibility when they come forward to speak against him.

We pray for his wife who, in negligence and denial, allows this to happen.

Bless her soul.

We pray for the families he touched with your guidance, Lord, for we all have demons you instilled in us.

Tonight, Lord, we also pray for the men and women sleeping in those cardboard boxes on the sides of your roads.

We pray for the homosexuals, and the bisexuals, and the confused, because you made them this way.

Lord, we pray for those who are so blinded by your light that they cannot see what is blatantly in front of them.

We pray for the murderers and the depressed and the psychotic.

We pray for the sick children who die of cancer every day.

We pray, Lord.

For you.

You made us in your image.

You who inspires us to hate one another.

You who will not accept the very things you created.

You who allows evil people to succeed with no repercussions for their wickedness.

You who gave us your Son and then walked away.

You who made us in your image.

That, God, was probably the worst thing you could have done.

I thank you for the plans you make for us.

Even though we never wanted you to,

You sent your Son to die,

Not so that we could be saved

But so that you could be the one to save.

Pray for us, my Lord.

We are going to need it.

At Sea

July 4, 2017

It's like being sick, but nothing's physically wrong. Occasionally
your fever breaks and you can think clearly, but it never really goes
away. You can't sleep because your mind doesn't shut off. You're
overthinking everything and taking it personally. Then you start to
sweat, and you feel self-conscious about that, so you sweat more.

You wake up and go through the motions, but you're
somewhere else entirely. You're not here or there, you're
somewhere in between, and it's this thick, suffocating,
endless fog you just can't seem to navigate through.

There's no motivation or will to move or talk or
care about anything, but you have to try.

Every movement is painful, and you can't talk. You wake up in the
middle of tasks that you don't remember being assigned. The only
burst of energy comes from being reprimanded for being in the
wrong or wanting to get whatever it is done so you can go back to
your hole of despair and self-pity and hope they'll pity you too.

But pity isn't what you want.

All you can do is try to fake it. Appear normal so
you avoid attention, so you don't have to talk, even
though that's what you desperately want to do.

Your body is numb, and your blood turns into thoughts,
and you don't know whether you need to scream or punch
or throw things, and you envision doing all of it in front of
everyone just to show how you feel. But you don't.

You explode inside your mind and your body. Then you blink, and
you're just sitting there pathetically while everyone else carries on.
You try to blot out your thoughts with music while you
chain-smoke cigarettes, hoping they'll do you some good,
and praying to God that *no one* will bother you.
You see every look toward you as a threat, certain that those who are
looking at you see you for what you're feeling. It makes you paranoid,
but when they look away, you feel saddened that they've passed you
over. You find it funny because you don't even know these people.
You think about home and connections and things you're
missing and mishaps you should have been there for.
Your brothers and sisters are failing, but you can't
reach them, and they won't talk to you or write you.
Your mom is in hell, and you can't help her.
Your fiancée is at home all alone, taking care of things and trying
to be financially and emotionally strong for both of you, but you
can feel her worry and sadness through the emails she writes, and
you know you're the cause of that pain, so you almost just want to
stop emailing her back until you're better. But it's the only way you
can vent about anything, at the very least to someone you know
will listen and care and not just tell you to suck it up and keep
working, or to someone who's paid to listen and "care" and give
you some verse from a religious text you don't even believe in.
It's like desperately reaching out for a hand to hold, but you want
to sit inside your shell and try to wait out the storm inside you.
Then you think about how contradictory that
is, and that drives you even crazier.
You don't see anyone around you, understanding this
pain over nothing, so you just sit and wait it out.
Obviously you're miserable, but not even you are sure why.
There are the things everyone else is going through
too; so why are you different from them?
Are you just weak?

What is your purpose?

What's the point of being here when you hate everything about this place? The people, the lack of freedom, the work, the infrastructure, everything.

You think about how much of a waste of time this all is. Seeing places while you're under curfew like a child. Wasting your precious youth on greasing and greasing and greasing equipment you don't care about. Investing time into something that won't even be around in another ten years. But you will be.

The dreams you have for yourself and your family are all you've got. When you think about achieving them, the path just seems so frivolous and tiring that those thoughts aren't of any use to your mood.

You could be there right now building your relationships and spending time where it matters. Yet, you're here.

Wasting away.

You think about how much better things would be if you could change certain things, but you have no voice here.

You watch higher-ups and authorities with their coffee and self-righteousness. You can't tell if you hate them or admire them. You lean toward hate because they make your life so much harder than it has to be over petty bullshit.

You can't say anything (because, again, you have no voice) because you're here to serve and listen and think what they want you to.

They expect you to lead but won't let you because they're the leaders. One voice out of five thousand can't change shit in a regulated system. It causes more grief than it fixes. Useless.

July 5, 2017

Suicide is a lingering thought. Not necessarily to end it all but just to show people that that's where you're at. Maybe not to end your life. Risking your life to end this place.

You think about jumping off the side and going for a swim, but the fear that they won't turn back or that no one will see you keeps you from doing it.

You don't want to be alone, but you can't prevent yourself from being that way. You see yourself and your problems as meager and insignificant, as a burden to those around you.

This is the heart of what is driving you crazy. You don't want to be a burden, but you can't help but be.

Even your closest friend doesn't know what to say to you.

Is this a depression episode?

Are my meds working?

Should I double the dose?

Why can't I just feel normal and have normal connections with people?

You notice you're the only one on the smoke pit, most of the time, not engaging in interaction, and you just wonder, *What's wrong with me?*

Is this the ship or the depression?

Is it the stress, or the people, or everything combined?

How long before you actually snap?

You just feel like screaming. All. The. Time.

Your self-image is slowly turning into garbage as you try to fit in among the people you are forced to live among. They tell you that you're too skinny. Then a chair falls apart underneath you, and it makes you feel heavy.

All in all, you just lose your appetite.

You didn't eat any food on the Fourth of July out of the indignation that,
Really? The most they could do for us is give us a fake Fourth of July meal?
Maybe if you starve you'll actually start to feel something other than this numbness.
You don't eat for a couple of days and finally break.
Now when you eat, you feel like that fat kid in the corner eating by himself while everybody watches.
You know you're not, but that's just how you see it.
These little thoughts and insecurities keep grabbing at you and pulling you under.
From the tone of your skin to how badly you smell halfway through the day,
This is not what you signed up for.
Nobody told you about the overpowering and pretentious feel of this system.
Nobody told you how it would affect your self-image and self-worth.
"You need to act like an adult."
Well, then, stop treating us like children.
So many limitations, and yet you're somehow expected to exceed expectations.
Inconsistency is the only consistency that exists, and it's overwhelming.
Maybe if you stop drinking water, you'll pass out and end up in medical for a few days, where no one can bother you.
Maybe if you cut yourself open, the same thing will happen.
Maybe that wouldn't be as good.
Too much attention.
Goodbye, privacy.

July 6, 2017

You spend a lot of time watching people. You wonder if they're
capable of compassion or not and, if so, to what extent.
You wonder if the more time you spend here means the
less compassion you feel because you are so caught up in
trying to get over whatever this phase of your life is.
You talk to your supervisor about making a general discharge
happen and getting you the hell out of here. It makes you
feel relief, but it also makes you feel disappointment, because
you are not strong enough to finish what you started.
You feel weak even though your friends and family are encouraging you.
You don't want to let them down, but you don't know
what else to do. Your supervisor asks you how he
can help you, and honestly you don't know.
What can anyone do for you?
Why can't you do anything for yourself?

July 7, 2017

Today you cried for the first time in a long time. You shut yourself
in a room where nobody would come looking for you and just
did your best to let it out. It felt like a pathetic attempt to regain
your strength, but it helped. For a whole twenty minutes.

July 8, 2017

Does nobody else see this?
Are you being petty?

Are you the problem?

Do you serve a purpose, or are you purposely serving?

You just want to be done with all of it. But hey,

guess what? You don't have a choice.

You don't decide your fate here.

You can't even decide how to get your hair cut.

People are flaky in both their words and their actions.

The couple of people you have close to you, who know what you're going

through, will make plans and then never follow through with them.

No follow-up, nothing.

Need to talk at this particular time? No-show.

That's when this thought of invisibility kicks in. Like

voicing an opinion or thought and somebody just talks

over you like you weren't even there to begin with.

Just as you start really opening up to someone, the phone rings.

You start again, and there's a knock at the door.

You start again, and someone random is invited into the

conversation, and suddenly the topic (which, you understand, was

slightly uncomfortable) just fades away without follow-up.

The moment's no longer right.

The attention isn't there, so what's the point?

You have yet to find someone who keeps up with

what they say, without being forced to do so.

You do your best.

If you don't show, there's a good reason.

You would do just about anything for the people you care about.

Why are you so easily cast aside and forgotten?

July 9, 2017

It's your birthday today, but you had to openly

say it was for anyone to take notice.

No one's made any kind of effort to make it special in any way.

You had to bring it up to make plans with
your best friend. He didn't show.
After that, you made plans with your other friend, and surprise, surprise!
She was a no-show as well.
It's petty, you understand, but it would be
nice to be noticed today of all days.
You're tired of trying so hard. You wish you wouldn't. Maybe
it's out of self-interest and the need to be noticed.
Maybe it's just your nature.

July 11, 2017

Sometimes you wonder if you had to learn to be human.

You notice you tend to take a quality you see that you like in someone else and subconsciously mold it into your psyche.

You feel like most, if not all, of your phrases and gestures, and how you interact in certain situations, come from movies, or television shows, or your friends who are creative enough to come up with shit themselves.

You've always been good at imitating.

What you are finding, though, is that the things you dislike most about yourself generally come from you.

It's like living inside a million different people.

Every now and then the real you pokes its head out and says something off or does something disagreeable and clumsy.

Then you're left to snap back into the mask and laugh it off like that wasn't really you who did it.

Feeling uncomfortable in your own skin.

This is probably a topic that you could rant on and on about.

But now everything is fine, so it's back to the daily grind.

Over and over and over again.

Angels

I'm having these horrifying dreams
Of posttraumatic things,
Like the demands of the King
Coming down in a scream,

Angels reprimanding
My actions from before.
"You think we wanted this for you?"
They ask, as if I were a chore.

"How could you ever let this be?"
I am lost as I rejoice.
"You are not lost, just confused."
As if I had a choice.

"We've been standing right beside you
Regardless of your self-inflicted fiends.
People you hold on to
Are just an end to the means.

"You are not worth understanding,"
They tell me, as for escape they yearn.
"You are no longer blessed
With the privilege of our concern.

"While that may sound condescending,
We are certain of every word.
You will never be ascending."
Of this I am assured.

These dreams, these dreams
Of catastrophic things,
Like the sound of falling angels
Pleading for their burning wings.

They howl and scowl
As they shun me for my way.
I am but their witness
As their King on Judgment Day.

Sorry, Not Sorry

Sorry, not sorry for my inclination
But for your observation.
This conversation
Is killing me.

So, go now.
Retreat because you cannot beat me.
And I know you won't agree,
But please know that I will never, ever be
Exactly what you want of me.

Your disappointment
Doesn't bother me at all.
You can smother and beseech me,
But I will never let you see
The very best part of who I want to be.

I'm sorry, not sorry
For this observation,
But your inclination and,
This conversation bores me.
So, please, just let me be.

I know you will fight me,
But it doesn't faze me in the slightest.
You can try your best to erase me,
But you will not
Until you've seen me at my brightest.

Marks

Wounds become scars
Under the day's sun,
Under the night's stars.
Day by day by day
I've learned a lot from these marks.
To not have gone so fruitfully
In my past, in my mistakes.
It's worth living and dying from this toxicity.
Is the misery worth savoring?
Is the pain worth contemplating?
I've come to understand that
It's what makes life living,
To show you have feelings,
To watch these monsters swallow your heart.
They eat with unnerving indignity.
It's setting the ground beneath me apart.
Falling into shoes I no longer fit,
It's seen I no longer care.
But just like these monsters, it eats away at me.
But it is myself and I who are feasting.
I'm ready to let go.
I'm ready to leave.
Show me a path I can follow
So I can take responsibility for what I weave
While the tears fall and shatter the ground.
I cannot help but think

The sun has fled for good.
The light no longer holds a link.
Love is a shadow
Like the light that has fled,
Just like a switch in my head,
Turning off the spark that makes me, me.
The pain fills these veins.
I've let you get in too deep.
I'm bored of feeling.
Give me something I can keep.
Go your separate way, and I'll go mine.
I'm no longer looking back at this.
I've become numb to everyone's touch.
But now hopefully you understand you were the catalyst.

Spit

You're standing there,
And you don't know why
I just spit
Right in your fucking eye.

All I asked for
Was your damn attention,
And while I have it
I have something to mention.

Your wicked lies
And your putrid cries
To justify your useless life
Make me want to spit rather than scream.

You're just not worth the wasted breath to me.

It'll never mean anything
If you kick and fight the words I sing.
It's just the giant principle of the thing,
Like the thought that made you think you're king.

It just makes me want to spit rather than scream.
You just don't mean a goddamn thing to me.

I just can't seem to convince you.
It doesn't matter what I say or do.
I guess that I just can't get through.
All the bullshit that you put everyone through—

I hope at least you've learned your fucking place.
You've lost this life's eternal race.
Standing silent now finally
As you're wiping spit off your face.

Selfish

Call me selfish,
Call me needy.
It's what I want,
But you consider it greedy

To have a hand to hold,
A voice to speak,
An ear to listen.
And what you see is cataclysm.

Trust me when I say this:

You are not Jesus Christ.
You are not perfect.
Your faults glisten
In the light from the sun.

You are just not something
I choose to believe in.

Yet you call me flawed,
Call me Satan,
Tell me that my wants,
My needs, should all be taken.

I just want you to know
That I feel sorry for you,
For this is what
You were destined to do,

To stomp around this world
Like its weight is beneath you.
But little do you know,
Sometime soon it will begin to crush you.

If you're as big as you think,
Why do you stoop so low?
You are not justified
To judge me like you know,

Yet here you are to crucify,
Here you are to rectify.
Maybe you should look inside
Instead of causing others to hide.

You are not the Messiah.
I am not a pariah.
We were meant to share the world,
Not destroy it,
Not own it.
Now who's being selfish?
The one who sees the world?
Or the one who seeks to rule it?

Soul Eater

I'll never see
This unsubstantial cross to bear.
The wear and tear
Just isn't justified.

We're horrified by the way
You cut these binds.
How can she?
How can I?

Every heart you stake,
Every breath you take,
Every scene you make,
Made worthless

By all the
Irrevocable lies,
Intangible cries,
And untraceable ties.

Yes, these are the things that bite.
Now you look in my eyes while
They cannibalize.
How can she?
How could I?

You swallow them whole
Like you don't have a soul.
And that is fine;
You can come take mine.

Just look into my eyes,
Believe in all my lies,
Listen to the cries
Of everyone I've swallowed whole.

You don't have a soul,
So come take mine.
How could she?
How could I?

Drown

I never meant
To let anybody down.
I've just got to try
To turn this shit around.

Mental breakdowns
Are the only consistency left inside me,
And they rain so consistently.
I'm drowning; don't come after me.

I can't hide anything from you.
You won't ever let me be.
While I was torn on the inside,
There was nothing you couldn't see.

I'm just afraid to pull you under,
Afraid you'll drown with me.
The bottom of the ocean will be lonely,
But I don't want your company.

I always thought I could be somebody,
But I never wanted to drag you down with me,
Because all you wanted was to be somebody.
All this time, and you haven't given up on me.

You see my flaws on the outside,
Make me believe that I can change.
For what it's worth, I'm trying,
But it might be better off this way.

I'm just afraid to pull you under,
Afraid you'll drown with me.
But if the bottom of the ocean suits you,
I could use the company.

Thread

Can't you see I'm hanging on by a thread?
Every now and then I'm starting to see red.
This place has got me feeling that this is the real me,
But really, it's not who I want to be.

Lately I've been feeling antisocial
When the time had come for connection to be crucial.
But I know why I had to isolate.
I just don't like the way that bitter people taste.

There's a fiendish devil in the air that I can't stand.
It's running through my veins and into my hands.
It sharpens teeth on people's pain,
Knowing well there's nothing to gain.

A sanity I can't redeem.
It makes me want to scream.
I cannot sleep at all at night,
Faced with visions of knots so tight

Around my wrists, around my neck.
Lever ready for the hole in the deck.
The noose is tied; it's time to drop dead.
All that's left is a single thread.

Wrote It

Waking up in my bones,
I will not be leaving here alone.
When the sweat drips from my charcoaled skin,

I'll still be there to let you in.

Weekend's absurd.
I'll not take another word.
Heart breaks in fault's taste.
I will make many more mistakes.

Kingdoms will fall.
I'll be there to see it all.
Fire and coals and flesh;
I'll be there at your behest.

I'm my bones I know it.
With this skin I'll show it.
Break me in or blow it.
It's by your design; I just wrote it.

Prismed

Giving up on my intuition,
It's created such a cataclysm.
Locked inside such a great divide,
Light closing in and off this prism.

You see I've gone so far
And come back with nothing but truth,
From when the lies and the fallacies
Altered and corrupted my youth.

The stars desperately scream out,
Dying for the light from the world to shine.
Yet here we are extinguishing our own flames,
None of which are fit to take blame.

After such an inclined fate,
One is only left to claw at and rake
Fragments of all that is left of me,
Wondering, *Where is the rest of me?*

I am scattered into shards of glass,
Breaking skin on the toes of people I pass
And the people I've grow to come close to,
But where have they gone to?

Light reflects off this prism.
It passes right on through,
Never touching the heart and mind
I thought to put faith into.

Creation

This is my creation.
This is my resolve.
This how I make the bad things
In my life dissolve.

This is my obsession.
This is my recollection.
This how I make memories ride
On into consecration.

When I'm feeling empty,
When I find myself in rage,
I turn around
And I fill this empty page.

This is my religion.
This is revolution.
This is me deciding where my life
Becomes evolution.

Daylight

Sweating and climbing
Up this steep mountain ridge,
Almost to the top,
Almost to the light,
Until the ledge I hold goes loose
And I'm falling back into the dark.

Daylight gets away from me.
Never-ending incline is all I see.
The devil's ninety degrees.
God's unnerving disease.

So, I work my way back up.
Inch by inch I climb,
Praying for some assistance,
Praying for something I need.
Almost to the summit,
I slip back into the dark,

Where daylight speeds away from me,
Where darkness is all I see.
The devil's ninety-degree angle,
God's unwavering eye.

It's upon me, and I see
This shimmering wave

Destined to heal this sickness,
About to relieve me of this climb.
But God is unwavering;
He seeks only to destroy.

Maybe the devil's ninety degrees
Is just where God put me
For this life,
For all life,
For my life.
For this life,
Take this knife.
Drive into this life.

Into the dark
Again I go,
Trembling, fading,
Until this life

Is nothing but ledges and ridges,
Nothing left but this climb,
Nothing left but the dark,
Nothing left but this.

Heights

I can't escape the sight.
From so up high here,
The wind is giving fight,
And I let go of all I fear.

Falling from the heights
Into catastrophic dreams,
Passing through life in flights,
Ripping memories at the seams,

I've seen the things I've done.
Having fallen through the world, I felt
The warmth of a wrathful sun
Burning the hand that I was dealt.

This was supposed to be a happy one,
Hopeful, joyful, whole,
But I've climbed to the top
And fallen just the same.

Speech Impediment

I don't know why
I say the things I do.
The things I have that are worth saying never work each other through.
I've never been so disconnected from myself.
Words and thoughts left to collect dust on the shelf.
Doing my best to never give a damn,
Slowly realizing this is not who I am.
So, the thoughts that began are driven under
Until they erupt and crash like thunder.
Now everything comes out all at once,
Clawing and pushing to make its way into eardrums.
The words come and then fall away,
Scratching inside like demons at play.
And I am left with the energy that they create.
There's nothing more to do but think about hate.
Coming from inside, stuck in a daydream,
Praying for an excuse to go hide away and scream.
Maybe someone will hear. Maybe someone will listen.
Maybe they'll think that it's just a condition.
Yet again I'm sick inside my head,
Thinking about things better left unsaid.

Cope

Another night gone.
Finding it hard to stay strong.
Starting to get sick
Of this same old song,
What do you do when
You've lost all hope.
Your sobs are mute.
You start to choke.
Tell me, how do you cope?
It's hard to get lost in a daydream
When they all remind you
Of a lost youth's gleam.
Recognizing it's gone,
Just sing the same old song.
When the day has
Weighed its length,
How do you keep up your strength?
When your emotions go blank,
Numb, and cold,
Tell me, how do you cope?

Bedtime Ritual

It's nights like tonight
I can't sleep,
Thinking about all the things
That I keep
Like a friend long gone
And a preacher
Who took my faith from me.

It's been a long road,
A lot of bumps along the way.
A crash or two
Just to start anew.
Tomorrow's always a new day.

My brain and my body
Just can't seem to blend
When the things that I want
Can't be justified.

Closed eyes just aren't enough
When there's so much behind them,
Making it tough
To be so stagnant

When there's just so much
That should be reprimanded.

So, I just lie in the silence,
In the self-induced blindness,
Waiting for my eyes and my body
To succumb to the darkness.

Reflection

It's like a reflection in a window.
I can see the world outside,
But I'm in the way of myself.
When it gets dark, the focus
Is on me.
I change before I realize
The change is through.
I wish I was wrong.
I wish I was hopeless.
I wish I was young.
I wish I had defenses.
I wish I had skin,
Skin harder than diamonds.
I wish I had the will
To block out all this numbness.

Owoah, owoah, owoah, owoah.

You can try to fake it,
But try and try,
You'll never make it.
You wish and you dream.
You struggle, you fight.
But the end of the day

Always meets the end of the night.
I wish I could fake it.
I wish I could make it.
I wish I had meaning.
I wish I had feelings.
I can't argue with nothing,
Yet I stand here just yelling
At the top of my lungs,
"Will someone please help me?"
Oh no,
On my own.
Oh no,
Time to reap what you've sown.

Owoah, owoah, oh no, oh no.

Is this window a mirror?
Could it make it any clearer?
Using myself as the pawn,
Trying to play on,
Is it really worth fighting?
As the time proves we're dying,
Am I stuck in this world?
Or is it stuck with me?
Help me.
I won't.

Daydreams

Midnight smoke
In a spotless daydream.
Listening to words
That make my thoughts gleam.
Simmering in cold fluorescent light,
Wishing for action to take flight.
These eyes are shimmering.
Haunted by cut teeth
And a will to live.
Ever bearing an overdramatic vision,
One of pure precision.
Never at fault
While midnight smoke
Invades my unblemished daydreams.
Enveloping my deepest desires,
It rises from internal empires.
Opening eyes to close from the sting,
Billowing in what should've been
A spotless daydream.

Where Did I Go?

I am a shadow of what I used to be.
If you knew me then,
You wouldn't hesitate to agree.
When there was still light inside me that shone through.
Now it's been shrouded,
But it tries, desperately, to bleed through.
I used to be fearless and stand up
To sing and write and do things like this,
But in this prison, there is no room for such things.

I used to be wise.
I used to give without regard for myself.
But now if it's not in my self-interest,
I put it back on the shelf.
I used to be compassionate for those who lost and wished them the best,
But now you may as well just rip my heart from my chest.

I would've bled, would've died for any of my friends,
But now I look around and don't see any of them.
I used to see inspiration in the kind acts of others.
Now all I see are the foolish acts of my "brothers."

I used to be free to be whoever I wanted to be.
Now the time has gone by
All too quickly,
And all I am now is a shadow
Of what I used to be.
If you used to know me,
It'd be painfully clear to see
I won't hesitate to disagree.

Glass

I stare at myself.
I can't help but think,
Who is this in front of me?
Who are you?
Punch in the face.
The mirror shatters.
The broken pieces of glass fall.
My feet now bleed, and so do my arms.
My hands smell of disgust.
My body shakes with betrayal.
And somewhere in this wave of pain
I remind myself of who I was,
Of who I used to want to be.

Now I sit at my desk until
I make these words make sense—

From heart to mind,
From mind to hands—

Until they don't flow right anymore.
Nothing flows the way it should.
Once again, I have forgotten this face.

Maybe the pain will wash it away.
Maybe I'll find myself in the strain,

From cut to blood,

From blood to scab,

Until I'm ready to open back up again.

In Hell

I am my own hell.
It is what I make.
I have stumbled on a path
Most would never take.
It is my will to move through
The flames and all the fire.
Just as one goes out,
Another rises higher.
Trapped inside my soul,
Pushing out the rest,
All the things that don't matter.
Get them off my chest.
My hope is living through
All the messes that I make,
Eventually burning out
So this path is one no one will take.
I'm alive to be beaten.
Withhold it all inside.
Violence has no virtue.
I will not be the one who died.
The stigma of a mass.
Hell is what awaits,
But hell is the ground we walk,
The thing our mind creates.

I am strong enough
To walk this alone.
You may only see weakness,
But my path has been shown.
I can take what comes.
There's nothing of worth to say.
There's a reason for everything.
Hell is not red; it's gray.
I will not be remembered
When I have finally gone.
The ones who helped me when I stumbled
Will say I was strong.

At the End

From the grass to the grave
Marks the road I have paved,
And while it is worn and rugged,
It has held promise
For those following it.
They will see where I've stood
And look at the beauty I've seen.
They will see where I've wandered
And see the unkindly demises of those around me.
Some footprints
Are left on the road;
Others, I've erased.
For the sake of others,
I keep moving on.
As the days go by,
Watch as these prints grow.
See as I've become wiser with them.
You can see this in the details.
Step by step as the weeks go by,
See the prints of the many beside mine.
These are the people who have touched my life,
As I have theirs.
Some go on until mine stop.
Some go on a different route.
I cannot blame them,
For they have a right to go as they please

Just as much as I do.
So, I keep moving on,
Even as the years go by.
Time slips away
Like sand in the desert.
While it may scatter joyfully in the wind,
There's an infinite supply of it.
I have come to know this.
Because while my tracks haven't been covered,
They seem to float away.
And it goes on day by day.
But I move on
As my life goes by
Until the day that I die.